Getting To Know...

Nature's Children

RED FOX

Merebeth Switzer

PUBLISHER	Joseph R. DeVarennes
PUBLICATION DIRECTOR	Kenneth H. Pearson
MANAGING EDITOR	Valerie Wyatt
SERIES ADVISOR	Merebeth Switzer
SERIES CONSULTANT	Michael Singleton
CONSULTANTS	Ross James
	Kay McKeever
	Dr. Audrey N. Tomera
ADVISORS	Roger Aubin
	Robert Furlonger
	Gaston Lavoie
EDITORIAL SUPERVISOR	Jocelyn Smyth
PRODUCTION MANAGER	Ernest Homewood
PRODUCTION ASSISTANTS	Penelope Moir
	Brock Piper

EDITORS

Katherine Farris   Anne Minguet-Patocka
Sandra Gulland   Sarah Reid
Cristel Kleitsch   Cathy Ripley
Elizabeth MacLeod   Eleanor Tourtel
Pamela Martin   Karin Velcheff

PHOTO EDITORS	Bill Ivy
	Don Markle
DESIGN	Annette Tatchell
CARTOGRAPHER	Jane Davie
PUBLICATION ADMINISTRATION	Kathy Kishimoto
	Monique Lemonnier

ARTISTS

Marianne Collins   Greg Ruhl
Pat Ivy   Mary Theberge

This series is approved and recommended by the Federation of Ontario Naturalists.

OJ JP PG OL FP

Canadian Cataloguing in Publication Data

BB
Switzer, Merebeth
  Red fox

(Getting to know—nature's children)
Includes index.
ISBN 0-7172-1904-6

1. Red fox—Juvenile literature.
I. Title. II. Series.

QL737.C22S97 1985   j599.74'442   C85-098732-6

Have you ever wondered . . .

Think of a story you know that has a fox in it. What is the fox like? In the stories about Brer Rabbit, Brer Fox plays tricks on Brer Rabbit all the time. The fox in *Pinocchio* is always getting children into all sorts of trouble.

Sneaky, sly troublemakers—that is how foxes appear in many stories. But real foxes do not deserve this bad reputation. They may seem to be sneaky or sly at times, but they are just being clever in order to hunt for food and escape enemies.

Read on to find out more about a very smart fox, the Red Fox.

Shy, smart and clever are a few ways to describe the Red Fox—handsome, too!

Meet a Red Fox Cub

Red Fox cubs love to play. Their mother brings home special treats for her growing cubs. Bones, feathers and sticks become toys for the foxes to chew, tug and fight over.

The cubs are not big, but they make loud squeals. These noisy balls of fur have not yet learned that a good hunter is a quiet hunter. But their play is teaching them other lessons, such as how to grab and hold on to prey. These are lessons that will come in handy when the young foxes must hunt for themselves.

With those big ears even a fox cub can hear a mouse squeaking in the grass up to 90 metres (300 feet) away.

Red Fox

Coyote

Wolf

A Relative for Rover

You might not be surprised to learn that the Red Fox has several fox cousins—the Arctic Fox, the Gray Fox, the African Fennec Fox, the Kit Fox and the Swift Fox. But would you have guessed that the Red Fox is also related to the Timber Wolf, the coyote and even to dogs?

There are more Red Foxes than any other type of fox. Red Foxes live throughout most of North America and are also found across all of Europe, most of Asia and even in parts of northern Africa, India and Japan.

Where Red Foxes live in North America.

A Surprise for Settlers

When the pioneers first arrived in North America, they cleared the land for farms. To get away from people, many wild animals moved deeper into the wilderness. But the Red Fox stayed. The open fields, pastures and crops of the new settlers made a good hunting ground full of mice and other small animals. Empty woodchuck dens could be made a good home for raising a Red Fox's family, and farm woodlots sheltered the Red Fox from winter wind and snow. The early pioneers created a perfect home for foxes! Soon there were many more Red Foxes than there had been before the settlers arrived.

The Red Fox is most active at night, but is sometimes seen in early morning or late afternoon.

Sizing Up the Fox

The Red Fox weighs about as much as a small dog, and it is not much taller than a Bassett Hound. Its beautiful bushy tail is almost as long as the rest of its body.

The male fox, or dog, is usually larger than the female, or vixen. Red Foxes are also larger in northern areas than they are in southern areas. In the north, the extra weight protects the fox from the cold because its body does not lose heat as quickly. The thick winter fur of a northern fox makes it look bigger too.

One of the first things you notice about the Red Fox is its tail—it's long and very bushy.

A Fancy Dresser

The Red Fox is a very elegant looking animal. It even has black fur on its legs that looks like black stockings.

Are Red Foxes red? Not always. Just as you and your friends have different colors of hair—blond or red or brown or black—so too do Red Foxes. In fact, sometimes young foxes in the same family have different colors of fur.

The Red Fox's fur is most often a reddish brown, but it may also be a beautiful silver or black. Many Red Foxes have buff or white patches on their body—on the tip of their tail, chest, belly or even on their lips. Some Red Foxes even have a dark-brown or black cross pattern on their backs and shoulders. These are called cross foxes.

By late fall the Red Fox has already grown its thick winter coat. That way it will stay toasty warm when the first snow falls.

15

Snoozing in a Snowbank

How would you keep warm if you had to sleep outdoors all winter long? A good sleeping bag and blankets would help. A fox does not have blankets to keep it warm. Instead it has a double thick fur coat. Long, smooth guard hairs cover the warm, thick underfur of the fox's coat. The guard hairs act like a waterproof windbreaker, keeping out water and cold wind. The woolly underfur acts like long underwear, keeping the fox's body warm. On cold days, the fox looks for a place that is out of the wind, such as a hollow at the edge of a snowbank. There it curls up into a tight ball and folds its furry tail over its nose and paws. The snow acts like a blanket and helps to keep the fox warm.

Brrr—you might not find it cozy curled up in the snow, but with its long thick fur, the Red Fox certainly does.

The Tracks of a Traveler

The Red Fox hunts for food all winter long. Every night it may travel for several hours searching for food. If a fox got cold feet in winter, it would not be able to hunt for the food it needs to live. To keep its feet warm, the fox has fur between its toes. This fur also gives the fox a better grip when running over slippery ice or snow. If you find fox tracks, look closely and you may be able to see the marks left by these hairs.

Snow is no problem if you have furry footpads to keep your feet warm.

Outfoxed by a Fox

Some animals climb trees for safety, but not the Red Fox. It has other tricks to help it escape enemies.

A Red Fox will lead its enemy on a merry chase through a manure pile, along a carefully balanced log and into a patch of raspberries. Each game of chase may be different—perhaps a short swim in a pond or a mad dash across a highway. If you were a bear trying to catch a fox, would you follow it through such an obstacle course?

The Red Fox is famous for "outfoxing" all who try to catch it, even humans. And it is because the Red Fox is so smart at getting away that it is known for being cunning, sly and crafty.

A Red Fox may not be able to waltz, but it sure can fox trot—up to 10 kilometres (6 miles) per hour.

Fox tracks

A Meal Everywhere

The Red Fox will eat almost anything. This is one of the reasons it has survived so well. The fox likes rabbits, voles, mice and other small rodents best, but it will also eat insects, snails, eggs and other things that it finds on its travels. If a fox is lucky enough to kill a large animal, it may bury the part it does not eat right away and save it for a meal later on. If meat is scarce, foxes will also eat wild fruits such as blueberries and apples.

The Red Fox can sniff out a mouse even when it is tunnelling under the snow.

Friend or Enemy?

Foxes sometimes hunt farm animals such as chickens and turkeys and steal eggs. This has given them a bad reputation among farmers. But foxes also help farmers by catching mice and other small animals that eat crops and ruin stored grain.

Looking for Clues

The fox uses its keen nose, sharp eyes and good ears to help it hunt. The movement of a rabbit hiding in the long grass, the sound of a mouse scurrying along a tunnel under the snow or the smell of a bird hidden in the bush are all clues that show the fox its next meal.

To catch a mouse, a Red Fox will pounce and trap it between its front paws just like a cat. Also, like a cat, a fox may sit without moving and wait for a long time before jumping on its prey.

A fox sometimes buries its food. It will come back to eat it later.

Teeth Like a Tree?

The fox's teeth stay hard and sharp because of a new layer of hard enamel that grows each year. Have you ever counted the rings on a tree stump to see how old the tree was? In the same way, scientists can tell how old a fox is by looking at one of its teeth. If a fox's tooth is cut in half, you can see a ring for each new layer of enamel. You can tell how old a fox is by counting the enamel rings on the tooth.

By studying fox teeth in this way scientists have found that many foxes die from disease or are killed by predators when they are young. Those foxes that learn to hunt and defend themselves will often live to be 12 or older.

Red Fox tooth

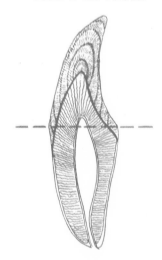

Cross-section showing enamel "age" rings.

A Red Fox has 42 teeth. How many can you count in this mouth?

Keep Out

Foxes "talk" to other foxes by using different barks and yelps, just as dogs do. Every now and then a fox might even howl.

But foxes do not always bark their messages. Sometimes they send silent messages to other foxes. How? The male fox urinates against trees and other upright objects. These "scent-posts" tell other foxes: "This territory is already taken."

If the intruder ignores this message, it may be in for a fight. Sometimes both foxes stand on their hind feet hitting each other with their front paws and biting at each other's muzzle.

To avoid being hurt, the weaker fox usually admits defeat quickly. Crouching close to the ground with its ears flat against its head, it wails a cry that says:"You're the boss."

After a victory, the "boss" fox may show off. It fluffs up its fur, making it look nearly twice as big as it really is. Then, with great majesty, it struts stiff-legged over to a scent-post and marks it. This tells the loser that it is time to make a quick exit.

Opposite page:

Stop. Look and listen. A Red Fox is a skillful hunter. It waits and watches its prey before pouncing.

31

Choosing a Mate

During mating season, several male foxes may compete to win a mate. They strut back and forth, trying to impress her. Sometimes two males may even fight for the female. In these fights the strongest animal wins. This means the babies it fathers are likely to be strong too.

Often the dog fox and vixen will stay together for all their lives. Sometimes a dog fox may have more than one mate, but there is usually one vixen who seems to be his favorite.

The fox pair have a hunting territory that is about the size of 70 city blocks. They will only share this territory with another dog fox if there are no babies to protect. Young foxes are too precious to trust around a stranger.

Often a fox will sit outside its den enjoying the warmth of the sun.

Borrowing a Burrow

When it is almost time for their cubs to be born, the Red Fox parents look for a good place to make a den.

Foxes are not great den diggers. They prefer to borrow an unused den abandoned by another animal, such as a woodchuck or badger. Sometimes, however, the mother fox must make do with a small cave, a hollow tree trunk or a thicket for a nursery. Although she will seldom dig her own den, she may make a burrow bigger by digging out rooms and adding entrances. Often one entrance faces south to help keep the den warm. Usually the den will have a small clearing at the main entrance. Later this will serve as a playground for the young fox cubs.

The foxes will use the same den year after year. They often make more than one den, so that the young can be moved quickly if there is danger.

Cut-away of Red Fox den.

Father Brings Home the Groceries

While the female fox finishes preparing the nursery den by lining it with leaves and grass the male brings home food for her. The vixen does not let him into the den, so he must leave her food outside the entrance. Any food she does not eat, she saves to eat later when the babies are born.

The Red Fox thrives in open grass and farmland where there is plenty of food.

Happy Birthday, Cubs!

Not long after the vixen settles into her den, the cubs are born. There are anywhere from four to nine cubs in a litter. The babies are helpless bundles of woolly brown fur, and they cannot see or hear for the first 10 days. They are content to sleep and nurse on their mother's rich milk.

During this time the dog fox brings food for the mother. He has not yet seen the cubs, but it will not be long before it is time for both the mother and father to share the hunting and the care of the youngsters.

As soon as the cub's eyes open and they start to crawl, the father is allowed into the den while the mother goes off to hunt. The mother fox never goes too far away. Her cubs are growing quickly, and they need to drink her milk often during the first weeks of life.

This happy cub gives mom a "welcome home" greeting.

Hello World!

By the time they are one month old the cubs are strong enough to leave the den for the first time. As they poke their heads into the sunshine, they blink furiously. This new world seems awfully bright after the dimness of the den.

Their mother keeps them in the small clearing in front of the den's main entrance. Like most of us, the cubs are shy in new places. If a leaf blows across the dirt, they go scurrying back inside. It is wise to be careful—a hungry bear or hawk may be nearby.

Time out. Red Fox cubs play hard but they know when to rest too.

Mini Meat Eaters

The cubs are now ready to eat their first meat. Like most babies, they start with baby food; their tiny teeth and young stomachs are not quite ready for big chunks of meat yet. To make this "baby food" the mother fox chews and swallows the meat. When her cubs cry for food, she brings it up. Eating is easier when food is first chewed and half-digested in this way. And it is also easier for the mother fox to carry food back to the den in her stomach rather than in her teeth.

These young cubs eagerly await their parents' return.

42

Learning Through Play

With each day, the cubs' play becomes rougher. They become braver and more daring in the world around them. A young fox learns how to hunt as it plays at fighting, chasing and stalking its brothers and sisters.

To practise hunting skills, the cubs pounce on butterflies and beetles. The mice and voles put at their feet by the mother and father become toys to fight over, toss and tear before eating. In this way the young foxes learn about the types of food to hunt.

The cubs grow up quickly. By early fall they are nearly three-quarters the size of their parents, and their adult coat of thick fur has grown in. They are also becoming skilled hunters.

Aw—come on. Let's play.

Family Goodbyes

Now it is time for all the foxes in the family to go their own way. The mother and father leave first, one after the other. They will not meet again until mating season the next spring. Then the young foxes set off on their own.

If the winter hunting is good, the brother and sister cubs may not go far from each other. But usually each young fox goes off alone often traveling more than 50 kilometres (30 miles) to find its own hunting territory.

The young Red Fox will not be alone for long. In January, it will be time for it to look for a mate and to start a family of its own.

Special Words

Burrow   A hole in the ground dug by an animal to be used as a home.

Cubs   Young foxes.

Den   Animal home.

Dog   The name for the male fox.

Enamel   The hard outer covering of teeth.

Guard hairs   Long coarse hairs that make up the outer layer of the fox's coat.

Litter   The name for all the cubs in a family.

Mating season   The time of year during which animals come together to produce young.

Nurse   To drink the mother's milk.

Predator   An animal that hunts other animals for food.

Prey   An animal hunted by another animal for food.

Territory   Area that an animal or group of animals lives in and often defends from other animals of the same kind.

Vixen   The name of a female fox.

INDEX

Cover Photo: Brian Milne (First Light Associated Photographers)
Photo Credits: Bill Ivy, pages 4, 32; Brian Milne (First Light Associated Photographers), pages 7, 9, 14, 18-19, 23, 27, 28, 30, 36-37, 38, 41, 45; Norman Lightfoot (Eco-Art Productions), pages 10-11, 20, 24-25; Arthur Savage, pages 13, 42-43; Wayne Lankinen (Valan Photos), page 17.

Getting To Know...

Nature's Children

RIVER OTTER

Laima Dingwall

PUBLISHER	Joseph R. DeVarennes
PUBLICATION DIRECTOR	Kenneth H. Pearson
MANAGING EDITOR	Valerie Wyatt
SERIES ADVISOR	Merebeth Switzer
SERIES CONSULTANT	Michael Singleton
CONSULTANTS	Ross James
	Kay McKeever
	Dr. Audrey N. Tomera
ADVISORS	Roger Aubin
	Robert Furlonger
	Gaston Lavoie
EDITORIAL SUPERVISOR	Jocelyn Smyth
PRODUCTION MANAGER	Ernest Homewood
PRODUCTION ASSISTANTS	Penelope Moir
	Brock Piper

EDITORS

Katherine Farris	Anne Minguet-Patocka
Sandra Gulland	Sarah Reid
Cristel Kleitsch	Cathy Ripley
Elizabeth MacLeod	Eleanor Tourtel
Pamela Martin	Karin Velcheff

PHOTO EDITORS	Bill Ivy
	Don Markle
DESIGN	Annette Tatchell
CARTOGRAPHER	Jane Davie
PUBLICATION ADMINISTRATION	Kathy Kishimoto
	Monique Lemonnier

ARTISTS

Marianne Collins	Greg Ruhl
Pat Ivy	Mary Theberge

This series is approved and recommended by the Federation of Ontario Naturalists.

Canadian Cataloguing in Publication Data

Dingwall, Laima, 1953-
  River otters

(Getting to know—nature's children)
Includes index.
ISBN 0-7172-1908-9

1. Otters—Juvenile literature.
1. Lutra canadensis—Juvenile literature.
I. Title. II. Series.

QL737.C25D56 1985   j599.74'47   C85-098733-4

Have you ever wondered . . .

What furry little animal can be seen sliding down muddy hills on its belly at top speed, hiding pebbles on the bank of a stream and juggling a chunk of food in its paws? If you guessed the River Otter, you are right.

A family of otters will sometimes play hide and seek in the tall grass at the edge of a pond. In winter they might even try to slide *up* a snowy hill!

Learning about River Otters is almost as much fun as watching their antics. Read on to find out more about these amazing, playful little animals.

Meet the Relatives

The River Otter belongs to the weasel family. Its North American relatives include the mink, fisher, ermine, badger, wolverine, skunk and marten.

Weasels come in all sizes. The Least Weasel is no bigger than a banana—about 20 centimetres (8 inches) long, while the Sea Otter can grow up to almost 1.5 metres (5 feet) long and weigh as much as a ten-year-old child. In between is the River Otter.

The average Male River Otter weighs about eight kilograms (18 pounds) and measures a little over one metre (3 feet) from the tip of its nose to the end of its tail. Female River Otters are slightly smaller.

No matter how big or small they are, weasels have one thing in common. All of them make a strong sweet-smelling liquid called "musk" in two glands under their tail. The River Otter, like other weasels, uses this musk at mating time and to mark its territory. And like its close cousin the skunk, the River Otter sometimes sprays musk when it is alarmed. Fortunately the otter's musk is not as stinky as the skunk's.

Opposite page:

Though mainly active at night, the River Otter may venture out of its den during the day—that is if there are no people about.

River Otter Country

River Otters are found throughout most of North America from northern Canada to the southern United States. Close relatives of the North American River Otter live throughout much of South America, Europe and Asia.

Not all River Otters live in rivers. They make their homes in forests, on the prairies and the northern tundra and even in high mountains—as long as there is water nearby. A stream, a pond, a lake, a large marsh or a coastal bay makes a good River Otter home.

The shaded area of this map shows where North American River Otters live.

Water Lovers

The River Otter is as at home in the water as you are on land. It is an excellent swimmer and uses several different ''swimming strokes'' to help it get around. It often glides lazily along on its stomach, pushing now and then with one foot. Occasionally it might flip onto its back or side and float for a while.

At other times the River Otter moves in a snake-like way. Swimming on its belly, it dives and surfaces, dives and surfaces. First you see its head, then you see its tail, then its head, then its tail and so on.

Underwater antics.

Follow the Leader

A family of otters sometimes plays follow the leader. When the first otter dives underwater, the second in line comes to the surface. Meanwhile, the third otter dives and the last one surfaces. People have watched this sight in amazement, thinking they have come upon a huge water serpent.

River Otter underwater.

Follow the leader.

Diving Champion

The River Otter dives underwater to find food, escape from enemies, get to its den or just to play. It can stay under for four minutes or even longer before coming up to the surface for a breath of air. How? It slows down its heart rate so that the oxygen in its lungs is used up more slowly and therefore lasts longer.

When a River Otter is in a hurry underwater, it tucks its front feet close to its chest and its back feet close to its tail and ripples its body up and down. Swimming underwater in this way, the otter can reach speeds of up to 11 kilometres (7 miles) per hour.

A River Otter can move through the water as fast as a canoeist.

Made for Water Living

The River Otter's body is well suited to all this swimming and diving. It has a sleek streamlined shape to help it cut through the water quickly and webbed feet to supply the paddle power. It uses its big back feet to do most of the work and holds its front feet close to its body.

When it is underwater the River Otter sometimes needs to make sharp turns to keep up with fish it is trying to catch. It uses its long thin tail as a rudder to help it change directions in a hurry.

Hind foot

The River Otter uses its flattened tail to help steer itself through the water.

Keeping the Water Out

The River Otter has a sleek fur coat that is not only warm—it is waterproof too! The otter's coat is actually two coats. Long, stiff guard hairs shed water, while short underfur keeps in body heat.

The otter's nose and ears are waterproof too. Its broad, black nose has its own built-in "nose plugs." These nose plugs are folds of skin that automatically cover the otter's nostrils when it dives underwater. No water gets into its tiny round ears either. It has built-in "ear plugs—folds of skin that close over the inner ear to keep water out.

The River Otter's outer coat is nearly waterproof.

Land Sprinter

At first glance the River Otter looks clumsy and awkward on land. But although its legs are short and stubby, they are powerful. The otter can gallop so fast that, over a short distance, it can outrun a man.

Usually, though, a River Otter pokes slowly along the banks of its home stream, river or lake. It searches for food on land as well as in the water. The size of its feeding territory depends on the amount of food available. If food is scarce, the territory will be large. If food is plentiful, the territory will be smaller.

An otter may travel a long way from its burrow in search of food.

Big Appetite

The River Otter is not a fussy eater. It will eat small land animals such as muskrats, shrews and young beavers. But it catches most of its food in the water. A River Otter will eat almost anything that swims or floats—fish, frogs, tadpoles, turtles, insects and even ducks and other birds. Perhaps its favorite treats are the crayfish that live on the bottom of rivers and ponds.

To find crayfish and other bottom-dwellers, the otter dives all the way down and does a handstand. Then it pokes its nose into cracks, under rocks, between logs or even into the mud. Its stiff bristly nose whiskers feel around in these nooks and crannies until they touch something. When this happens, nerves at the end of the whiskers send a "food!" message to the otter's brain. And the otter digs in.

The River Otter usually feeds just after dusk and then again before dawn.

An otter's whiskers are an important part of its fishing tackle.

Dainty Eater

You will never see a River Otter gobbling down its food. When it has caught its dinner, it carefully carries the food to shore in its mouth or in its hand-like front paws. Then it takes small bites and chews carefully until the food is ground into tiny pieces. It must do this because it has a narrow throat. If the food is not in small chunks, the otter might choke on it.

Nibbling in this way, a full-grown otter will eat about one and a half kilograms (3 pounds) of food a day. That is about the same as 12 large hamburgers.

Fresh crab makes a tasty meal for a hungry River Otter.

A Cozy Home

The River Otter snoozes away most of the daylight hours in a den that has been abandoned by a beaver, muskrat or other animal. Sometimes the den is between boulders along the shore or under roots of fallen trees. Or it might be a comfortable place in a thicket of marsh weeds.

As soon as the River Otter moves in, it starts to make improvements in its borrowed den. It covers the floor with dried leaves, bark or moss to make a cozy bed. It sometimes hollows out a separate room to one side to use as a toilet. And it usually makes sure it has two entrances—one underwater, the other on the ground. That way it can always dart out one entrance if an enemy comes in the other.

Like most of us, otters enjoy sunbathing.

Life Under the Ice

For a long time scientists thought that River Otters slept most of the winter because they were only seen on very mild days. No wonder they thought that. Although River Otters are active all winter long, they spend much of their time under the ice and snow and so are rarely seen.

When a river or pond freezes over, the otter can still fish for food under the ice. It comes up for air at breathing holes or breathes from pockets of air trapped under the ice. After a food excursion under the ice, the otter snuggles back into its cozy den.

When it travels above the ice, the otter often tunnels under the snow rather than walking through it. That is because its legs are so short. If it tried to walk through deep snow, it might get stuck.

Crossing ice is not a problem for the otter. Tufts of hair between its toes both keep its feet warm and prevent it from slipping.

Opposite page:
Winter is a good time for overland journeys.

River Otter Talk

If you walk near a pond or river and hear what sounds like a loud cough, you might be near a River Otter. The otter blows through its nose, making a snorting cough-like sound, when it is startled or frightened. This may be the otter's way of clearing its nostrils so that it can smell the air better. Or it may be a way of telling other River Otters that danger is nearby. Some people think it is just a gasp of surprise.

There is no mistaking the sound of an angry River Otter, especially when it is face to face with an enemy, such as a lynx or other big cat. The otter opens its mouth wide to show all its strong teeth and screams loudly. That tells the enemy: "Watch out or I will bite!" Most animals take this warning seriously and retreat. If they do not, the otter will fight fiercely to defend itself.

The most common sounds a River Otter makes are quiet chuckling "huh-huh-huh" sounds and a soft birdlike "chirp chirp chirp." Those happy sounds are friendly otter-to-otter talk.

Fun and Games

It is impossible not to smile when you see a River Otter playing—it seems to be having so much fun!

The River Otter sometimes picks up pebbles, twigs and shells and juggles them in its front paws. It might even balance a leaf on its nose. Or it might dive to the bottom of the pond, find a stone, swim to the surface, float on its back and play with the stone in its paws.

If the River Otter drops the stone, the game does not end. It just dives underwater again to find it. But on the way down it might be distracted by a fish and chase it for a while. Or it might simply chase its own tail around and around.

Few animals are as playful as the River Otter.

33

Family Antics

There are plenty of high jinks when all the otters in a family get together. They chase each other along the shore and into the water, rolling and tumbling together in a bunch. Or they slide down slippery mud or grass-covered hills with front legs outstretched. The best hills for sliding are those near the river. Then the slide ends with a big splash.

River Otters like sliding so much that they will even do it without a hill. On level ground they will jump, jump, jump s-l-i-d-e—three short jumps and one long slide.

The otters' games do not stop when the snow falls. In fact otters love nothing more than tobogganing down a snow-covered slope on their stomachs. Sometimes a family of River Otters will play a wintertime version of hide and seek. One otter dives and tunnels under the deep snow, while another one jumps, rolls around and pokes its nose into the snow, looking for its hidden playmate.

Mating Time

The River Otter mates in late winter or early spring. At that time, the male makes musk in two glands under its tail. He leaves this musk smell around his territory. It warns other males to stay away and attracts females. The female also leaves a musk smell to tell males that she is ready to mate.

Once a male River Otter finds a mate, the two otters play together. They chase one another in and out of the water, rolling and spinning as they go. After they have mated they go their separate ways. But although they do not live together, the male stays close to his mate's den.

River Otter Birthday

The mother otter turns her den into a nursery by lining it with plenty of dry leaves and soft grass. She usually has two or three babies in early spring, but as many as five babies can be born at the same time.

A newborn River Otter is tiny—about the size of a baby kitten. It weighs just over 100 grams (4 ounces) and measures barely 28 centimetres (11 inches) from the tip of its nose to the end of its tail. It is covered with short fuzzy fur and has short whiskers around its nose.

The newborn otter cannot see or hear because its eyes are shut and its tiny round ears are sealed. They will not open until the baby is about 35 days old.

Sometimes you have to S-T-R-E-T-C-H to take a good look around.

Life in the Den and Out

The baby otters spend their early weeks in the den. When they are not nursing on their mother's milk, they sleep in a heap beside her or tussle with each other in play fights.

The River Otter mother only leaves her babies after dark, when she goes out for a short time to find food for herself. Even then she stays within listening distance and hurries back as soon as she can.

When the otter babies are about three months old, the mother lets them explore the world outside the den. By this time, the babies each weigh close to one and a half kilograms (3 pounds).

They stagger out of the den and try out their legs. Running is a problem. Their legs are still weak and wobbly, and they tumble and fall over their own feet and over each other.

Swimming Lessons

One of the first lessons the River Otter mother teaches her babies once they leave the den is how to swim. And that is not easy. The tricky part is getting the babies into the water in the first place.

Sometimes mother otter tries to coax her babies into the water with gentle nose-nudging. Other times she swims out into the pond and chirps for her babies to follow. Usually the babies will not have any part of this. They stand on the shore and refuse to get wet. Then the mother has no choice but to grab her babies one at a time by the scruff of the neck, tow them out into the middle of the pond and then let go. At first the babies just bob around on the surface, but soon they learn to swim.

Nature's water babies.

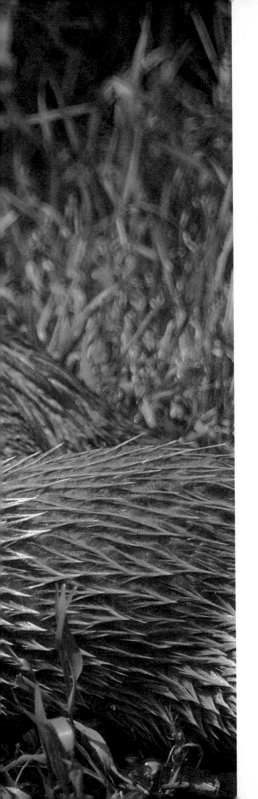

Fast Learners

In a few days the babies are so at home in the water that they follow their mother on her dives. They watch as she probes with her paws and whiskers on the bottom of the pond for crayfish and other treats. And they try to keep up when she swims after fish. The babies are fast learners and are soon catching their own dinners.

One Big Happy Family

By the fall, the young River Otters are about six months old and almost as big as their mother. Until this time they are raised by their mother alone. Then her mate joins her and they both look after the young.

The River Otter family spends the fall and winter together. In the spring, when the young otters are almost one year old, they leave their parents. But they do not wander far away. The young usually make their dens quite near their first home so there are always lots of otters nearby ready to play.

Special Words

Den Animal home.

Guard hairs Long coarse hairs that make up the outer layer of the otter's coat.

Marsh A flat area of land covered with shallow water.

Mate To come together to produce young.

Musk A powerful smelling liquid produced by the otter to mark its territory and attract a mate.

Nostrils The openings that allow air into the nose.

Nursing Drinking the mother's milk.

Territory Area that an animal or group of animals lives in and often defends against animals of the same kind.

Tundra A treeless region of the Arctic.

INDEX

Cover Photo: Brian Milne (Valan Photos)

Photo Credits: Brian Milne (First Light Associated Photographers), pages 4, 19, 27, 30; J.A. Wilkinson (Valan Photos), pages 7, 41, 42; Dennis Schmidt (Valan Photos), page 8; Bill Ivy, page 11; R.C. Simpson (Valan Photos), page 12; J.D. Markou (Valan Photos), page 15; Barry Ranford, page 16; Tim Fitzharris (First Light Associated Photographers), pages 20, 24; T.W. Hall (Parks Canada), page 23; J.D. Taylor (Miller Services), pages 28, 32; Thomas Kitchin (Valan Photos), page 35; Stephen J. Krasemann (Valan Photos), page 36; M.J. Johnson (Valan Photos), pages 39, 44.